Association American Art

Valuable Modern Paintings and Sculpture

Belonging to the Estate of George F. Tyler

Association American Art

Valuable Modern Paintings and Sculpture
Belonging to the Estate of George F. Tyler

ISBN/EAN: 9783744673280

Printed in Europe, USA, Canada, Australia, Japan

Cover: Foto ©Thomas Meinert / pixelio.de

More available books at **www.hansebooks.com**

EXECUTORS' SALE

GEORGE F. TYLER

Valuable Modern Paintings

AMERICAN ART GALLERIES
MADISON SQUARE SOUTH
NEW YORK

COROT   ZAMACOIS   DIAZ

PASINI   TROYON   BOUGUEREAU

CATALOGUE

OF

VALUABLE MODERN PAINTINGS AND SCULPTURE

BELONGING TO THE ESTATE OF

GEORGE F. TYLER, Esq., Deceased

PHILADELPHIA

TO BE SOLD BY ORDER OF EXECUTORS

ON FRIDAY EVENING, APRIL 9TH

AT 8 O'CLOCK

AT THE AMERICAN ART GALLERIES.

MADISON SQUARE SOUTH

WHERE THE PAINTINGS AND SCULPTURE WILL
BE ON FREE VIEW FROM MONDAY, APRIL 5TH,
UNTIL AFTERNOON OF SALE, INCLUSIVE

THOMAS E. KIRBY   AMERICAN ART ASSOCIATION.
AUCTIONEER   MANAGERS

NEW YORK
1897

CONDITIONS OF SALE.

1. The highest Bidder to be the Buyer, and if any dispute arise between two or more Bidders, the Lot so in dispute shall be immediately put up again and re-sold.

2. The Purchasers to give their names and addresses, and to pay down a cash deposit, or the whole of the Purchase-money, *if required*, in default of which the Lot or Lots so purchased to be immediately put up again and re-sold.

3. The Lots to be taken away at the Buyer's Expense and Risk *upon the conclusion of the Sale*, and the remainder of the Purchase-money to be absolutely paid, or otherwise settled for to the satisfaction of the Auctioneer, on or before delivery ; in default of which the undersigned will not hold themselves responsible if the Lots be lost, stolen, damaged, or destroyed, but they will be left at the sole risk of the Purchaser.

4. *The sale of any Article is not to be set aside on account of any error in the description, or imperfection. All articles are exposed for Public Exhibition one or more days, and are sold just as they are, without recourse.*

5. To prevent inaccuracy in delivery and inconvenience in the settlement of the Purchases, no Lot can, on any account, be removed during the Sale.

6. Upon failure to comply with the above conditions, the money deposited in part payment shall be forfeited; all Lots uncleared within three days from conclusion of Sale shall be re-sold by public or private Sale, without further notice, and the deficiency (if any) attending such re-sale shall be made good by the defaulter at this Sale, together with all charges attending the same. This Condition is without prejudice to the right of the Auctioneer or Managers to enforce the contract made at this Sale, without such re-sale, if they think fit.

THE AMERICAN ART ASSOCIATION,

MANAGERS.

THOMAS E. KIRBY,
Auctioneer.

CATALOGUE

SALE FRIDAY EVENING, APRIL 9th

BEGINNING AT 8 O'CLOCK

AT THE AMERICAN ART GALLERIES

1

DARGELAS (Henri) . . . . **France**

Born at Bordeaux, 1828. Pupil of Picot. Medals, Paris, 1867, 1881.

JOYS OF CHILDHOOD

Signed at the right. Height, 9 inches. Width, 6¼ inches.

2

SCHEERES (H.) . . . . . **Germany**

A MUSICAL CAVALIER

Signed at the left. Height, 7¼ inches. Width, 6 inches.

5

3

BROWN (J. G.), N. A. .   . United States

Born in England, 1831. Studied in Newcastle-on-Tyne and
at the Royal Scottish Academy, Edinburgh; later, with
Thomas Cummings, N. A., in New York. Eelcted member
of the National Academy, New York, 1863. Medals, Boston
and San Francisco. President of the American Water Color
Society. Honorary member of the Salmagundi Sketch Club.

THE YOUNG PEDDLER

Signed at the right, and dated 1865. Height, 9¼ inches. Width, 6¼ inches.

4

CHEVILLARD (V.) .   .   .   . France

Born in Italy of French parents. Medals, Paris, 1889 and
1891.

STARTING FOR A VISIT

Signed at the right. Height, 7 inches. Length, 9 inches.

5

GIRARDET (Karl) .   .   .   . France

Born at Locle, Switzerland, May 13, 1810. Pupil of Léon
Cognict, Paris. Medals, 1837, 1842; Grand Medal of Prussia, 1843; Member of Academy of Amsterdam, 1853.

ITALIAN WASHERWOMEN

Signed at the right. Height, 11 inches. Length, 18¼ inches.

6

BEARD (W. H.), N. A. . United States

Born in Painesville, Ohio, April 13, 1825. Animal painter; visited Europe in 1857, studied one summer in Düsseldorf, and sketched in Italy, Switzerland, and France. Elected N. A. in 1862.

RETURN OF THE PRODIGAL

Signed at the left, and dated 1865. Height, 14 inches. Length, 20 inches.

VAN SCHENDEL (Petrus) . Belgium

Born at Ter Heyden, North Brabant, April 21, 1806. Died at Brussels, December 28, 1870. History and *genre* painter. Pupil of Antwerp Academy under Van Bree. Medals, Amsterdam, Brussels, 1845, and Paris, 1844, 1847.

SELLING APPLES AT NIGHT

Signed on the right, and dated 1863. Height, 16 inches. Width, 12 inches.

PERALTA (Francisco) . . . Spain

Born in Seville, studied under Madrazo in Madrid, then visited Paris, and settled in Rome. Was showing great talent, when, through the defalcation of his banker, he lost his fortune, and became impaired in health through worriment. Returned to his native city, and died there, broken-hearted, in 1896.

SENTINEL ASLEEP

Signed at the left, and dated Rome, 1874. Height, 15½ inches. Length, 22 inches.

BIERSTADT (Albert), N. A.   United States

Born in Düsseldorf, Germany, January 7, 1830. Landscape painter. Brought by parents in 1831 to New Bedford, Mass., where his youth was spent. Began to paint in oils in 1851. Went to Düsseldorf in 1853 ; studied four years there and in Rome. On his return to the United States in 1857 he made a sketching tour in the Rocky Mountains, and from this and other visits to the West gathered materials for his most important pictures. Again visited Europe in 1867, 1878, and 1883. Elected N. A. in 1860. Medals in Austria, Germany, Bavaria, Belgium, and Paris. Legion of Honor, 1867. Order of St. Stanislaus, 1869.

WIND RIVER MOUNTAIN, NEBRASKA

Signed at the left, and dated 1862. Height, 12 inches. Length, 18 inches.

BROWN (J. G.), N. A. . . United States

Born at Durham, England, 1831. Studied at Newcastle-on-Tyne and in the Edinburgh Academy. Painted portraits in London, and in 1853 came to New York, where he studied at the National Academy of Design. While painting portraits in this city for a living, he cultivated an original style of *genre* which speedily attracted attention to him, and whose popularity led to his final adoption of this class of art. Became a member of the National Academy, 1863 ; is one of the founders and president of the American Water Color Society, member of the Artists' Fund Society, etc.

CROSSING SWEEPER

Signed at the left, and dated 1865. Height, 15½ inches. Width, 10½ inches.

CHAPLIN (Charles J.) . . . France

Born at Les Audelys, France, 1825. Pupil of the École des Beaux Arts, and largely employed in decorating public buildings of Paris, as well as portrait and figure painter. Medals, 1851, 1852, 1865. Legion of Honor, 1865 ; Officer, 1877. Died in Paris, 1891.

THE BATHER

Signed at the left. Height, 16 inches. Width, 10 inches.

12

VERSCHUUR (W.) . . . Holland

Born in Amsterdam, 1812. Died at Borden, July 4, 1874. Landscape and animal painter. Pupil of Pieter Gerardus van Os and of C. Steffelaar. Member of Amsterdam and Rotterdam Academies. Medals at Amsterdam, 1831, 1832, 1838 ; at The Hague, 1858, 1859; Officer of the Order of Oaken Crown, 1862.

HORSES IN WIND STORM

Signed at the right. Height, 11 inches. Length, 14½ inches.

13

VERBOECKHOVEN (Eugène J.) Belgium

Born in Warneton (West Flanders), July 8, 1799. Medals at Paris, 1824, 1841, 1855. Legion of Honor, 1845. Chevalier of the Orders of Leopold, St. Michael of Bavaria, and Christ of

Portugal. Decoration of the Iron Cross, Member of the Royal Academies of Belgium, Antwerp, and St. Petersburg. Died, 1881.

W 10. —

SHEEP IN STABLE

Signed at the right, and dated 1863. Height, 10¼ inches. Length, 14 inches.

14
BÉRAUD (Jean) . . . . . France

Born in St. Petersburg, of French parents, and studied art in Paris under Léon Bonnat. His first success was made by scenes of every-day life for the illustrated journals, characterized by much spirit and truth of drawing, and by pictures of the same class of subjects. As a portrait painter he has also achieved good standing. In 1882 he won his first medal at the Salon.

3 60. —

LEAVING THE MADELAINE

Signed at the left. Height, 9½ inches. Length, 12½ inches.

15
VERSCHUUR (W.) . . . Holland

Born in Amsterdam, 1812. Died at Borden, July 4, 1874. Landscape and animal painter. Pupil of Pieter Gerardus Van Os and of C. Steffelaar. Member of Amsterdam and Rotterdam Academies. Medals at Amsterdam, 1831, 1832, 1838; The Hague, 1858, 1859; Officer of the Order of Oaken Crown, 1862.

2 70. —

NOONDAY REST

Signed at the left. Height, 5½ inches. Length, 7½ inches.

CHEVILLARD (V.) . . . . France

Born in Italy of French parents. Medals at Paris, 1889 and 1891.

10.— LE MANDEMENT DE MONSEIGNEUR

Signed at the left. Height, 5 inches. Width, 4½ inches.

DE HAAS (J. H. L.) . . . Belgium

Born at Hedel, 1830. Pupil of P. van Os and of the Amsterdam Academy. A cattle painter of well-established reputation. His success dates from 1855, when he exhibited two large cattle pictures at the Salon in Paris. After that he exhibited every year, increasing his popularity, so that there are now very few collectors who do not know his work. *40.—* Medals and decorations he has in abundance.

A BULL

Signed at the right, and dated 1857. Height, 12 inches. Length, 16 inches.

HENRY (E. L.), N. A. . . United States

Born in Charleston, S. C., 1842. Studied in Philadelphia, at Pennsylvania Academy of Fine Arts, and with P. Weber; afterward in Paris, under Suisse and Courbet. First exhibited,

1863, at the National Academy.   Elected A. N. A., 1869;
N. A., 1870.

100.—

A SPANISH CATHEDRAL

Signed at the left, and dated 1870.   Height, 14 inches.   Width, 12 inches.

19

WILMS (Josef) . . . . Germany

60.—

Born at Bilk, near Düsseldorf, 1814.   Still-life and *genre*
painter.   Pupil of Düsseldorf Academy under Schadow and
Theodore Hildebrandt.

FRUIT, NUTS, AND GLASS OF WINE

Signed at the right, and dated 1863.   Height, 13½ inches.   Length, 16 inches.

20

PASINI (Alberto) . . . . . Italy

Born in Busseto, Italy.   Pupil of Ciceri.   Medals, Paris, 1859,
1863, 1864.   Grand Medal of Honor (Exposition Universelle),
1878.   Chevalier of the Legion of Honor, 1868.   Officer of the
same, 1878.   Medal at Vienna Exposition, 1873.   Knight of
the Order of Saints Maurice and Lazarus, and Officer of the
Orders of Turkey and Persia.   Honorary Professor of the
Academies of Parma and Turin.

" In the Chevalier Alberto Pasini we have an Italian who paints
the Orient as a Turk might who was born to its spirit and
nourished on its air.   From Ciceri he acquired his firm
draughtsmanship, from Isabey his color and bold and fluent
execution of the brush, and from Rousseau the deeper feeling
and sentiment of that master of landscape.   No man of our

time succeeds like him in realizing upon canvas the life and spirit of the Orient, its splendor of color, brilliancy of burning light, and barbaric sumptuousness of gorgeous pageantry.

ARAB GROUP, CONSTANTINOPLE

Signed at the right, and dated 1868. Height, 10 inches. Length, 18 inches.

21

MERLE (Hugues) . . . . France

Born at Saint Marcellin, France, 1822. Pupil of Léon Cogniet. Medals, 1861 and 1863. Legion of Honor, 1866. Died, 1881.

MOTHER AND CHILD

Signed at the left. Height, 16 inches. Length, 13 inches.

22

GIFFORD (Sanford R.), N. A.   United States

Born at Greenfield, N. Y., 1823. Graduate of Brown University, 1842. Pupil of J. R. Smith and the National Academy of Design, New York. Elected National Academician, 1854. Studied in Paris and Rome, 1855 to 1857. Travelled also in Italy, Greece, Syria, Egypt, and the Rocky Mountains. Died in New York, 1880. He was one of the first American painters to depart from the conventions of the old school and create a broader and higher style.

AUTUMN

Signed at the left, and dated 1862. Height, 16 inches. Length, 30 inches.

ROLFE (H. L.) . . . . England

FISH

Signed at the left, and dated 1864. Height, 18 inches. Length, 30 inches.

SONDERMANN (Hermann) . Germany

Born in Berlin, 1832. *Genre* and portrait painter. Pupil of Otto, 1851 to 1853 ; then studied in Antwerp, Paris, and under Jordan in Düsseldorf.

GRANDMOTHER'S TALES.

Signed at the right, and dated 1863. Height, 24 inches. Width, 21 inches.

HETZEL (George) . . United States

DEAD GAME

Signed at the left, and dated 1865. Height, 18 inches. Length, 24 inches.

BOUGUEREAU (William Adolphe), France

Born in La Rochelle, 1825. In 1842 he went to Paris and entered the studio of Picot, and later the École des Beaux-

Arts, where his progress was rapid. He gained the Prix de Rome in 1850, and then studied in Rome. Medals, Paris, 1855 (Exposition Universelle), 1857, 1867 (Exposition Universelle). Chevalier of the Legion of Honor, 1859. Member of the Institute of France, 1876. Officer of the Legion of Honor, 1876. Medal of Honor (Exposition Universelle), 1878. Knight of the Order of Leopold, 1881. Grand Medal of Honor, Paris, 1885. Medal of Honor, Antwerp, 1885.

RETURNING FROM THE HARVEST

Signed at the left. Height, 24½ inches. Width, 19 inches.

27

MAY (Edward Harrison) . United States

Born in England, 1824. Portrait, history, and *genre* painter. Taken to America when a child. Pupil of Daniel Huntington and Courture in Paris. Elected an A. N. A. in 1876, but rarely exhibited. Professional life spent chiefly in Europe. Died in Paris, 1895.

PORTRAIT OF A WOMAN

Signed at the left, dated Paris, 1875. Height, 26 inches. Width, 21½ inches.

28

BROWN (J. G.), N. A. . United States

Born at Durham, England, 1831. Studied at Newcastle-on-Tyne and in the Edinburgh Academy. Painted portraits in London, and in 1853 came to New York, where he studied at

15

the National Academy of Design. While painting portraits in this city for a living, he cultivated an original style of *genre* which speedily attracted attention to him, and whose popularity led to his final adoption of this class of art. Became a member of the National Academy, 1863 ; is one of the founders and President of the American Water Color Society, member of the Artists' Fund Society, etc.

STILL LIFE

Signed at the left, and dated 1865. Height, 26 inches. Width, 16 inches.

29
BOMPIANI (Roberto) . . . . Italy

A prominent artist of Rome, brother to Agusto Bompiani, also painter of *genre* subjects.

THE FAIR HARVESTER

Signed at the left, dated Rome, 1863. Height, 24 inches. Width, 19 inches.

30
VAN OS (G. J. J.) . . . . Holland

Born at The Hague, 1782. Died , Paris, 1861. Landscape, flower, fruit, and still-life painter. Son and pupil of Jan van Os. He took a medal in Amsterdam, 1809, and settled there. He painted also a great deal for the porcelain factory at Sèvres. His paintings are in museums of Amsterdam, The Hague, etc.

FRUITS AND FLOWERS

Signed at the right. Height, 35 inches. Width, 27½ inches.

31

GORGIANA (N.) . . . . Italy
AN ENGLISH GIRL
Signed at the left, and dated.1866. Height, 29 inches. Width, 24 inches.

32

SZERNER (W.) . . . . . Poland
COSSACK CAVALRY RECONNOITRING
Signed at the left centre. Height, 16 inches. Length, 32 inches.

33

ISABEY (Eugène Louis Gabriel) . France

The son of a famous master of miniature art, Eugène Isabey lived to overshadow his father's fame. He was born at Paris in 1804, and commenced his career as a painter of *genre*. He early began to experiment in marine painting as well, and during all his long career divided his labor between these two lines of subject. He received a first-class medal as early as 1824, and in 1827 was awarded another, the first being for a *genre* and the second for a marine picture. In 1830 his fortune was finally assured by his appointment as royal marine painter with the expedition to Algiers. His works were received into the most important museums of France, and collectors contended for them for private galleries. He had the Legion of Honor conferred upon him in 1832, and became an Officer in 1852. He died in 1886.

LEAVING THE CATHEDRAL
Signed at the right, and dated 1864. Height, 23½ inches. Width, 16½ inches.

17

DIAZ DE LA PEÑA, (N. V.) . Franc

Born at Bordeaux, August 21, 1808. His parents were ban
ished from Spain on account of political troubles, and at ten
years of age Diaz was left an orphan in a strange country
At fifteen years of age he was apprenticed to a maker of por
cclain, where his talent first displayed itself. He quarrelec
with and left his master, and subsequently spent several ycarı
in most bitter poverty. After his ability as a most wonderfu
colorist was recognized, Diaz painted and sold many pictures
working even too constantly, as if endeavoring by the accu
mulation of a vast fortune to avenge the poverty of his youth.
Medals, 1844, 1846, 1848. Legion of Honor, 1851. Died
from the bite of a viper, November 18, 1876. Diploma to the
Memory of Deccased Artists (Exposition Universelle), 1878.
"In the group of painters beyond the average, Diaz de la
Peña is the great artist of the fantastical. Anything serves
him as a pretext for bringing to light his marvellous aptitude
as a colorist. He dots the pond-side, where the sun gleams
with peasant girls, mere little red touches. In his sun-gilt
landscapes Diaz puts such figures as offered, by their cos
tumes, a pretext for the wealth of his palette. From the
Orient, as he passes through it, he only collects the remem
brances of silky stuffs and golden embroideries, spreading
forth their pride in the sun ; from Italy he only preserves the
method of the colorist Veronese, whom he often equals in the
attractiveness, if not in the conception, of his work. As for
mythology, it is merely his excuse for modelling in full im
pasto and in open daylight the nymphs and the Dianas."

MOORISH CHILDREN

Signed at the left. Height, 10⅜ inches. Length, 17 inches.

18

1000.—
B. B. Samuels

ZAMACOIS (Eduardo) . . . Spain

Born at Bilbao in 1842. Died in Madrid, January 14, 1871. *Genre* painter. Pupil at Bilbao of Balaco; then of Madrid Academy, under Frederieo de Madrazo; and in Paris, of Meissonier. Medals, Paris, 1867; Munieh, 1870.

"A Spaniard with the wit of a Frenchman, a painter with the satire of Goya and the art of his master Meissonier, it is no wonder that the *début* of Zamacois in 1863 was hailed by Paris as the rising of a new sun over the horizon of art. The artist was then twenty-three years of age, burning with the fire of youth and spurred by the daring of an audaeious and fecund brain. At each succeeding Salon his exhibits widened his popularity and augmented his reputation, whieh was crowned in 1870 by his 'Education of a Prinee,' a satire so bitter and scathing, yet withal so brilliant in its execution, that reprobation was disarmed by the genius of which it was the evidenee. The picture was the swan-song of the artist. He died in 1871, having scarcely turned his thirtieth year. The life-work that he left formed a series of gems, sparkling with wit and eolor, in whieh the influence of Meissonier showed in a certain decisiveness of handling, but which were thoroughly individual and unique."

ANTE–ROOM OF THE DUKE OF ALVA.

Signed at the left, and dated 1867. Height, 12¼ inches. Length, 16 inches.

36

WOUVERMAN (Attributed)

STABLE INTERIOR

Height, 17¼ inches. Length, 23¼ inches.

UNKNOWN
RECEPTION OF ST. CATHARINE
Height, 27½ inches. Width, 17½ inches.

FANFANI (E.) . . . . . Italy
RUTH AND REBECCA
(A PAIR)

Signed at the right and left. Height, 31½ inches. Width, 21½ inches.

TROYON (Constantine) . . . France

Troyon was born at Sèvres in 1810, and worked in the porcelain manufactory, as his father had done before him. Riocreux, the flower painter there, taught him to draw, and at twenty years Troyon was a student of landscape painting from nature, with some advice and encouragement from Roqueplan, whom he met on one of his sketching tours, and who became interested in him. It was as a landscape painter that Troyon made his *début* in the Salon of 1833, and in this walk he displayed a sentiment for light and color of the first order; but in 1847 he astonished the Salon, after a trip to Holland, where he had studied the old Dutch masters closely, with a cattle piece so splendid in spirit and so powerful in color and vivid realism, that his fame was established

20

at once. In 1849 he was decorated with the Legion of Honor, and the augmentation in the prices and the popularity of his works made him rapidly rich. The great school of French cattle painting, whose foundation Bracassat had laid, Troyon built up. He gave life and soul to the brutes he painted. His oxen have the grand movement of nature, his cows ruminate the cud and watch you with their soft eyes, his sheep bleat an appeal out of the canvas, and the dog which guards the flock or travels at the heel of the poacher or the gamekeeper only needs to bark to be alive. Poetry saturates his art—the humble rustic poetry which becomes majestic through its very simplicity. Troyon's color, his appreciation of light, and the ripeness and harmony of tone which characterize his pictures, were sustained to the last. He won medal after medal, at Salons and expositions, and enjoyed for nearly twenty years an uninterrupted course of honor and prosperity. Like Corot, he remained unmarried, content with his art, and helpful of the younger talents whom his genius attracted to him, and upon whom he made an impression which one sees reflected still in French art. Sixty masterpieces from his brush graced the Salon between 1833 and 1865, in which latter year his splendid career passed into a splendid memory.

LANDSCAPE AND CATTLE

Signed at the left. Height, 29 inches. Length, 37 inches.

40

COROT (J. B. C.) . . . . . France

Jean Baptiste Camille Corot was born in Paris, 1796, the son of a prosperous tradesman. Pupil of Michallon and Victor

Bertin, and travelled in Italy in 1826. Travelled much in France, painting from nature and creating a style out of his experiments. Although at first neglected by the public, his patrimonial fortune enabled him to live comfortably and paint to suit himself. He received medals, 1833, 1848, 1855, 1867 ; was given the Legion of Honor in 1846, and became an Officer in 1867. He died in Paris in 1875. The influence of Corot on the art of our time cannot be overestimated. He lifted landscape painting into the realm of idyllic poetry, just as Rousseau gave it a tragic, and Diaz a romantic significance. Each man painted according to his feelings. The spirit of the south which budded in Diaz, the melancholy of an un-happy life which darkened Rousseau, were replaced in Corot by a genial gayety of temperament which reflects itself in his works. He was one of the earliest of the men of 1830 to receive public recognition, and when success did come to him, it atoned for the neglect of the past.

LANDSCAPE AND LAKE

From the Corot sale, Paris, 1875.

Sealed with seal at the left. Height, 35½ inches. Length, 46 inches.

41

DE DREUX (Alfred) . . . . France

Born in Paris, 1812. Pupil of Léon Cogniet. Medals, 1834, 1844, 1848. Member of the Legion of Honor, 1857.

DOGS CHASING A CAT

Signed at the left, and dated 1857. Height, 39½ inches. Width, 29½ inches.

CANNICCI (G.) . . . . . Italy

MADONNA AND CHILD

Copy of the original painting, by F. Bartholomme, in St. Mark's, Florence.

Signed and dated 1866. Height, 45 inches. Width, 33 inches.

HAMILTON (James) . . United States

Born in Ireland, 1819. Brought to America as a child. Studied in Philadelphia. Spent 1854 and 1855 in London. Died, 1878.

A ROCKY COAST, SUNSET

Signed at the left. Height, 32¼ inches. Length, 50 inches.

HERZOG (Herrmann) . . United States

Born in the city of Bremen, and early exhibited an uncommon inclination and fitness for the pursuit of art. At the age of seventeen he entered the Düsseldorf Academy, at that time the most flourishing art school of Europe, as a pupil of Professor Schirmer. When, however, in 1854, that distinguished master was called to take charge of the Academy of Carlsruhe, the young artist became a private scholar of the great Norwegian landscape painter, Hans Gude, whose influence gave the final direction to his genius, and led him to make the first of those fruitful voyages to Norway which have had the result of linking his name with the beauties of that picturesque land, and making both known all over the world. In 1864, the only occasion on which he exhibited at the Paris Salon, his picture received *Mention Honorable,* and his work has subsequently been medalled at the Expositions of Liege, Brussels, and the Centennial in Philadelphia. Many of his paintings are in public museums and in the private collections of sovereigns. The Grand Duke of Oldenburg, Duke Ernest of Saxe-Coburg Gotha, the Emperor Alexander of Russia, the Countess of Flanders, and others, are among the royal and imperial amateurs who have purchased his pictures.

NORWEGIAN LANDSCAPE

Signed at the left, and dated 1864. Height, 32 inches. Length, 54 inches.

45

ROBBE (Louis) . . . . Belgium

Born November 17, 1806, at Courtray, Belgium. Was at first lawyer (1830) in Ghent, and in 1840 one of the syndics of Brussels. He entered the Academy of his native town, and in a few years had earned many medals and honors. In 1844 he was made a Knight of the Spanish Order of Charles III.; in 1845 a Knight of the Legion of Honor, and in 1863 an Officer of the Belgium Order of Leopold.

LANDSCAPE AND CATTLE

Signed at the left. Height, 32½ inches. Length, 50 inches.

LANDSCAPE, SHEEP, AND GOATS

Height, 29½ inches. Length, 44 inches.

47

MURILLO (after)

BEGGAR BOYS

(PAINTING ON PORCELAIN)

48

MEINVELT (C) . . . . Munich

BACCHANALIAN SUBJECT

AFTER RUBENS

(PAINTING ON PORCELAIN)

MARBLE STATUARY

49

IVES (C. B.) . . . . United States

A native of Connecticut, but for many years a resident of Rome. He made busts of General Scott, William H. Seward, and other noted persons. For the American Centen-

nial Exhibition he sent " Nursing the Infant Bacchus." He
was author of the statue of Trumbull, in marble, in front of
the new State House at Hartford, Conn.   Died, 1895.

Bust—ARIADNE

(WITH MARBLE PEDESTAL)

50

POWERS (Hiram) .   . ' . United States

Born at Woodstock, Vermont, July 29, 1805.   Died in Florence, Italy, June 27, 1873.
In 1817 his parents removed to Cincinnati, where he worked
with energy and industry at any mechanical employment that
came to hand.   He developed remarkable ingenuity in the
contrivance of figures moving by machinery to the accom-
paniment of music.   A bust of Napoleon, by Canova, having
come under his notice, he was excited by the desire to be-
come a sculptor, for which art he had had no further training
than was supplied by instruction in the taking of plaster casts
from models, in which he had been taught by a Prussian ac-
quaintance.   Assisted by Mr. Longworth, he went to Wash-
ington, and there found sufficient employment in making
busts to enable him to lay up a little money toward getting to
Italy.   Assisted by Colonel Preston and Mr. Longworth, he
went to Italy in 1837, and settled down into what was to
prove a life-long residence.   His work consisted largely in the
making of busts, in which field he gained a wide popularity
in Europe as well as in his native country.   In 1843 he pro-
duced the statue of the Greek Slave, a work which had an
immense success, fixed his reputation the world over, and

gave a great impetus to the slowly growing culture of art in this country. The question of slavery was just then taking on new importance in America, and Powers's Greek Slave played no small part in the fray. Mrs. Browning wrote a sonnet to the statue, and drew from it an argument for the doing away with all slavery.

> " Appeal, fair stone,
> From God's pure height of beauty, against man's wrong;
> Catch up in thy divine face not alone
> East griefs but West, and strike and shame the strong,
> By thunders of white silence overthrown."

100

Bust—PROSERPINE

(WITH MARBLE PEDESTAL)

Total $ 22.207.50

51

GIBSON (I.)

200

Statuette—EVE

52

ROSSI (C.) . . . . . . Milan

Bust—PSYCHE

(WITH MARBLE PEDESTAL)

27

53

Statuette—VENUS CALLIPICI

54
55
} *Please refer to Special Catalogue*

AMERICAN ART ASSOCIATION,

Managers

THOMAS E. KIRBY,

Auctioneer

www.ingramcontent.com/pod-product-compliance
Lightning Source LLC
Chambersburg PA
CBHW021609270326
41931CB00009B/1401

*9 7 8 3 3 3 7 3 0 0 7 8 4 *